# INTRODUCTION TO CIM & CAD

I0436090

## CAD:

A CAD system is a combination of hardware and software that enables engineer and architects to design everything from furniture to airplanes. In addition to the software, CAD systems require a high-quality graphics monitor, a mouse light pen or digitizing tablet for drawing; and a special printer or plotter for printing design specifications. CAD systems allow an engineer to view a design from any angle with the push of a button and to zoom in or out for close-ups and long distance views. In addition, the computer keeps track of design dependencies so that when the engineer changes one value, all other values that depend on it is automatically changes accordingly.

## Components of CAD system:

A CAD system can be considered as consisting of three major parts,

- Hardware : computer and i/o devices
- Application software : CAD package
- Operating system software and CPU.

In the CAD system, the functions of the CPU are as follows;

To receive information from the work station and display the output on a CRT screen. To read the data stored in a secondary memory storage unit. In addition to main memory circuits in CPU, secondary storage capacity is provided to reduce the cost of the main computer. The functions of the secondary storage unit area as follows: to create files related to the engineering drawing. To store CAD software and to store programs required to give instructions to output devices like plotters.

**Design related tasks;**

- Geometric Modeling
- Engineering analysis
- Design review and Evaluation
- Automated CAD drafting

**Geometric Modeling;**

During the geometric modeling computer converts the command into a mathematical model, stores it in the computer data files, and display it as an image on the CRT screen, object can be represented by geometric model by wireframe, surface or solid model.

**Wireframe Modeling;**

Wireframe modeling is a technique for representing 3D objects, in which all surfaces are visibly outlined in lines, including the opposite sides and all internal components that are normally hidden from view. Wireframe modeling is the least complex method for representing 3D images compared to surface and solid modeling.

## Surface Modeling;

A type of geometric modeling based on geometry only, in which all visible surfaces of a part are shown regardless of volume definition.

## Solid Modeling;

A type of geometric modeling based on solids in which all visible surfaces of a part are shown. In addition, solid modeling describes interior volume, mass and weight.

## Engineering Analysis;

Checking the designed object for its functionality is called as engineering analysis. In almost all the engineering design related projects some or the other analysis is required. It can be stress-strain calculations, heat transfer measurements or using differential equations to find the dynamic behavior of the system, which is being designed.

## Design review and Evaluation;

Review and Evaluation is checking whether the designed part has been designed properly or not and if they will fail in practical situations. It is very important part of the whole design process with CAD software the process of design review and evaluation has become much faster and convenient.

## Automated CAD Drafting;

Drafting is the process of making the drawings of the designed parts. After designing of the object its assembly and detail parts drawings have to be made which includes specifications of various materials also called as bill of materials used for the manufacturing the components of the object. Automated Drafting is one of the most important applications of the CAD software.

In this laboratory, we have used Pro/E version 4.0 CAD software for solid and assembly modeling.

# Pro Engineer

## Pro Engineer

Pro Engineer is the landmark product from PTC, USA. It is the first 3D modeling CAD system to incorporate extensive parametric, feature based, solid modeling.

## Pro E Solid Modeler

The three dimensional solid modeling approach in Pro/E provides the photo realistic visualization that can be understood even by the non technical members like marketing people. Other benefits in solid modeling approach are

- Mass property calculations
- Volumes and surface area calculations
- Interface checking etc.

## Parametric

Any model developed in Pro/E is parametric, i.e it is given by parameters or variable dimensions. Parametric can be defined as any set of physical properties whose values determine the characteristic or behavior of an object.The features provide

- Changing the model geometry by modifying the dimensions
- Interrelationship between features

- Parent-child relationship, feature reordering
- Presenting design intent.

**Feature based modeling:**

Pro/E geometry is composed of a series of easy to understand features. Pro/E allows building a model incrementally, adding individual features one at a time. By this feature based modeling we can obtain

- Flexible and reliable model by incrementing features one at time.

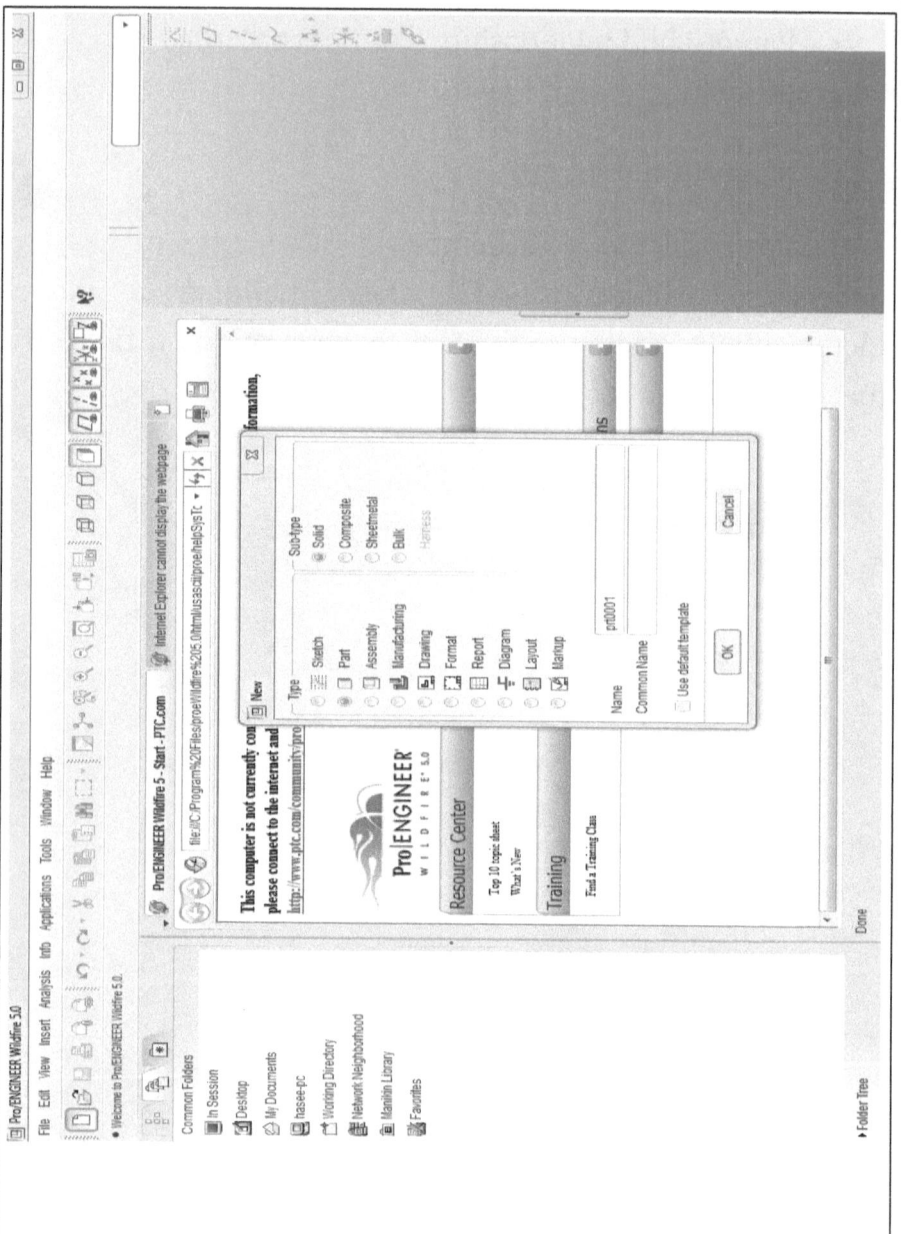

- Re-ordering and re-routing features as per requirements.

**Associative modeling:**

The part developed in Pro/E part model is also used in other modules like assembly, drawing, manufacturing etc. The associative modeling function provides,

- Change at a certain level automatically updated in all the levels.
- Bi-directional associative among drawing, modeling etc.

**Parent/child relationship:**

Parent/child relationships provide a powerful way to capture yours "design intent" into a model. Parent/child relationships are naturally created between features during the modeling process. When creating a feature, existing features that are referenced become parents to the new feature. Also, if the parent features are updated, the child features will automatically update accordingly.

**Commands used in Pro/E:**

**Part modeling:**

- **Extrude:**
  Extrusion is a method of defining three dimensional geometry by projecting a two dimensional section at a specified distance normal to the sketching plane.
- **Revolve:**
  The revolve tool creates a feature by revolving a sketched section around a centerline. Use the revolve tool as one of the basic creation methods that allows

you to create a revolved geometry as a solid surface, and to add or remove material.

- **Shell:**

    The shell feature hollows out the inside of the solid, leaving a shell of a specified wall thickness. It lets you specify a surface or surfaces that you want to remove from the shell.

- **Rib:**

    A rib feature is a thin or web protrusion that attaches to solid surfaces in you design. Typically, ribs are designed to strengthen parts in your design and are often used to prevent unwanted bending.

- **Draft:**

    The draft feature adds a draft angle between -$30^\circ$ and +$30^\circ$ to individual surface or to a series of surfaces.

- **Round:**

    Rounds are a type of edge treatment feature in which a radius is added to an edge or edges, an edge chain, or between surfaces.

- **Chamfer:**

    Chamfers are a type of feature where an edge or corner is beveled. There are two types of chamfer according to the type of placement reference selected.

    (a) Corner
    (b) Edge

- **Datum planes:**

Datum planes are used as reference on a part where one does not already exist. For example, you can sketcher or place feature on a datum plane when there is no other appropriate planer surface.

- **Datum point:**

    Datum points can be used as a construction element when modeling geometry or as a known point for conducting computations and model analysis.

- **Copy and paste:**

    The copy, paste, and paste special commands are used to duplicate and place features, geometry, curves, and edge chains. Using this functionality, you can copy and paste features between two different models or between two different versions of the same part.

- **Mirror:**

    The mirror tool enables you to create of features and geometry that are mirrored about a planer surface. You can use this tool to save time by mirroring simple parts into more complex designs.

- **Pattern:**

    Patters are used to create multiple instances of the selected feature by varying some specified dimensions. A pattern is parametrically controlled. Therefore, you can modify a pattern by changing pattern parameters, such as the number of instances, spacing between instances, and original feature dimensions. After creation, the whole pattern behaves as a single feature.

- **Sweep:**

    A sweep feature is created by sketching or selecting a trajectory and then sketching a section to follow along it.

- **Helical sweep:**

    The helical sweep is created by sweeping a section along a helical trajectory. The trajectory is defined by both the profile of the surface of revolution and the pitch.

- **Swept blend:**

    A swept blend requires a single trajectory and multiple sections. To define the origin trajectory of the swept blend, you can either sketch a curve or select a chain of datum curves or edges.

## Assembly:

- **Mate:**

    Use the mate constraint to position two surfaces or datum planes with their normal pointing at each other.

- **Angle:**

    Use the align constraint to make two planes coplanar, two axes coaxial, or two points coincident. You can align revolved surfaces or deges.

- **Insert:**

Use the insert constraint to insert one revolved surfaces into another revolved surface, making their respective axes coaxial. This constraint is useful when axes are unavailable or inconvenient for selection.

- **Tangent:**
  Use the tangent constraint to control the contact of two surfaces at their tangency. Keep in mind that this placement constraint functions like mate because it makes surfaces: it does not align them. An example of the use of this constraint is the contact surfaces or point between a cam and its actuator.
- **Fix:**
  Use the fix constraint to fix the current location of the component that was moved or packaged.
- **Point on surface:**
  Use the point on surface constraint to control the contact of a surface with a point. You can use part or assembly datum points, surface features, or datum planes, or part solid surfaces for reference.
- **Edge on surface:**
  Use the constraint to control the contact of a surface with a planer edge. You can use datum planes, planer part or assembly surface features, or any planer part solid surfaces.

# WEDGE BLOCK

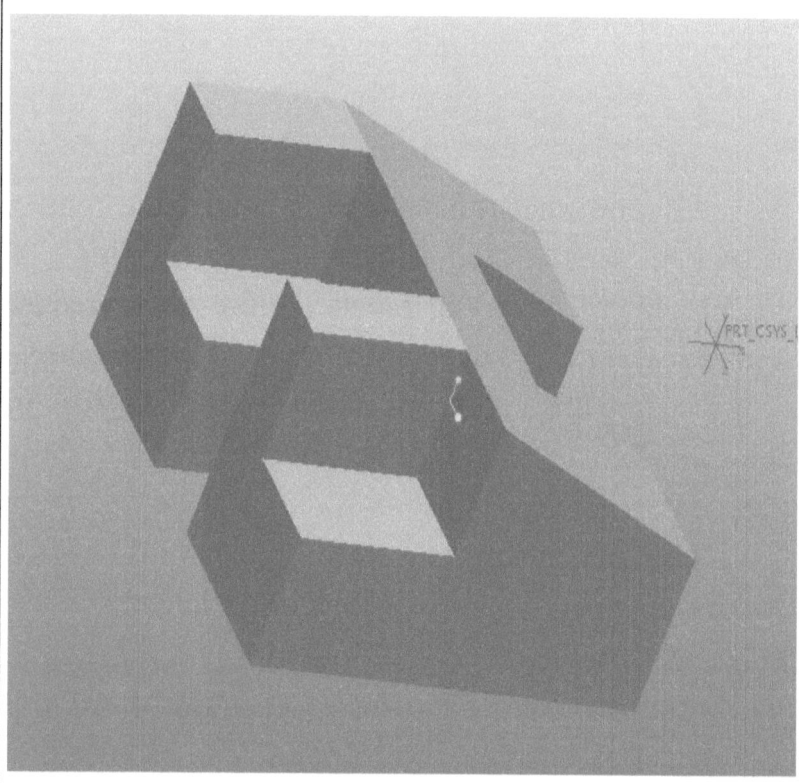

# SOLID MODELING OF WEDGE BLOCK

**Aim:**

To draw the given wedge block and design it by using the Pro/E software.

**Software used:**

- Pro/E Wildfire version 4.0

**Commands used:**

- Extrude
- Extrude cut
- Copy
- Pattern

**Procedure:**

**Step 1:**

- Open the Pro/E software
- Set working directory as desktop
- Open a new file
- Select part and remove the tick to change the default template into **mmns part solid.**

**Step 2:**

- Select the command extrude
- Define the placement and choose the right plane.

- Sketch the right new drawings as per dimensions.
- Now the extrusion is up to 50 mm and click ok.

# WEDGE BLOCK

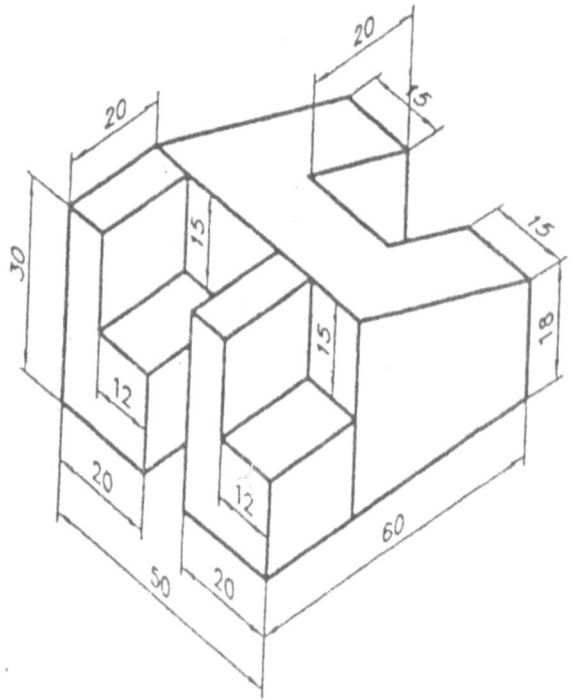

**ALL DIMENSIONS ARE IN MM.**

**Step3:**

- Select the extrude command
- Define the placement by selecting the top surface of extruded object
- Sketch a rectangle image of length 20 mm and breath 20 mm &click ok.
- Now the sketch is extruded up to the edge of previous extruded object.

**Step4:**

- Select the extrude command
- Define the placement by selecting the front plane.
- Sketch the image of L section as length 20 mm, height 30 mm and 12 mm & click ok.
- Now the image is extruded up to a distance of 20 mm before front image

**Step5:**

- Select the extruded object and now select pattern command.
- Pattern dialog box will appears
- Now, decide the distance of 30 mm.

**Result:**

Thus, the given wedge block is created by using Pro/E software.

# CORNER STOP

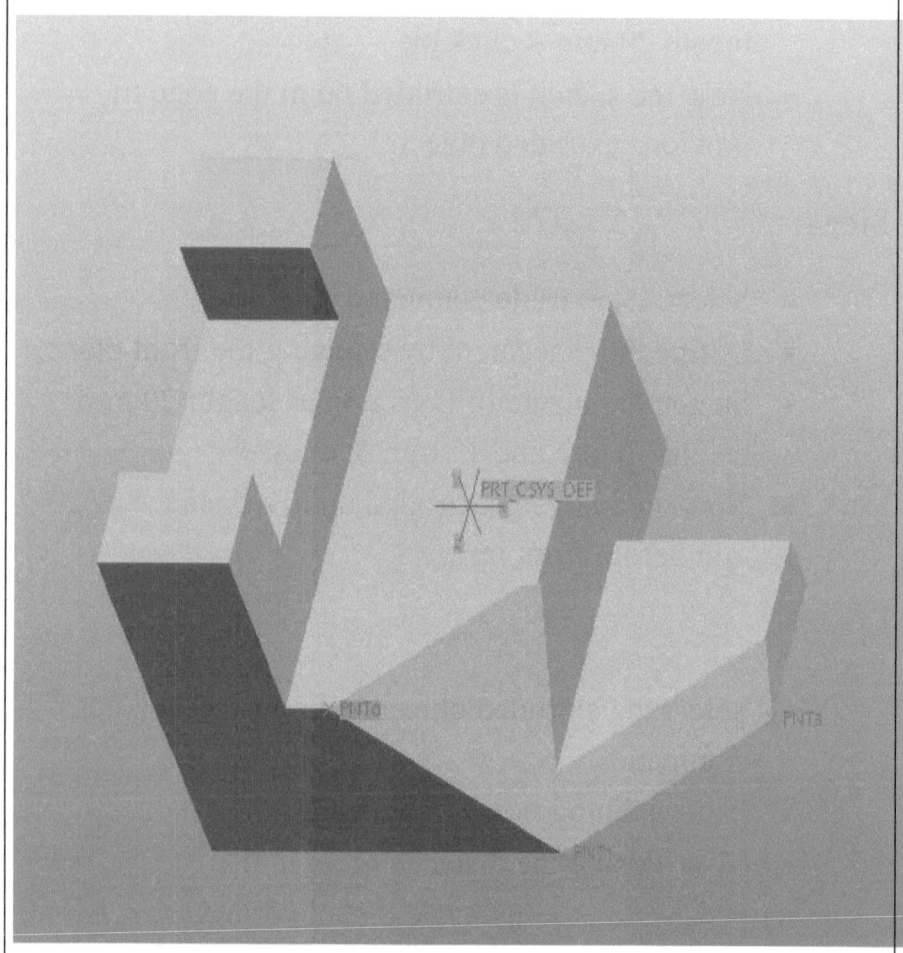

# SOLID MODELING OF CORNER STOP

**Aim:**

To draw the given corner stop by using the Pro/E software.

**Software used:**

- Pro/E software version 4.0

**Commands used:**

- Line
- Rectangle
- Extrude
- Extrude cut
- Multipoint
- Datum plane

**Procedure:**

**Step 1:**

- Open the Pro/E Wildfire 4.0
- Set the working directory
- Open the file-new-part
- Select the template **mmns part solid**

**Step 2:**

- Select extrude icon-placement-define
- Select the front plane &right orientation

- Use the line as sketching tool to sketch a front object as per dimensions and click ok.
- Now extrude and enter the value of 54 mm.
- Part 1 is extruded.

# CORNER STOP

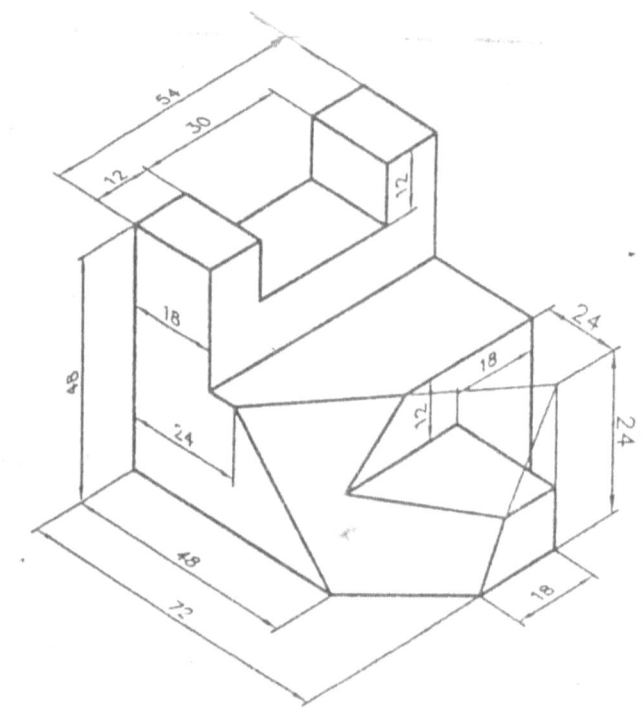

**ALL DIMENSIONS ARE IN MM**

**Step3:**

- Insert-extrude-placement
- Define the left side surface as reference with left orientation
- Draw a rectangle of 30×12 mm at a distance of 12 mm from anyone side edged top.
- Now click ok. Sketch & to the extrusion of 18 mm and click ok
- Now extrude cut is clicked and the material is removed.
- Part 1 with the cut surface is created.

**Step4:**

- Insert-extrude-placement-define
- Define the top surface as reference
- Cut the rectangular surface as per diagram given by sketching and click ok.
- Extrusion of 12 mm is given and cut is selected.
- Part 1with two cuts are created.

**Step5:**

- Use datum points to create a plane passing through the points.
- Now datum plane is mode to pass through that three points.
- Select cxtrude & placement is defined as the plane lastly drawn. A rectangle is sketched with should pass through datum point & click ok.
- Extrude cut is obtained at top of plane.

**Result:**

     Thus, the given corner stop is created by using Pro/E wildfire version 4.0 software.

# SUPPORT BRACKET

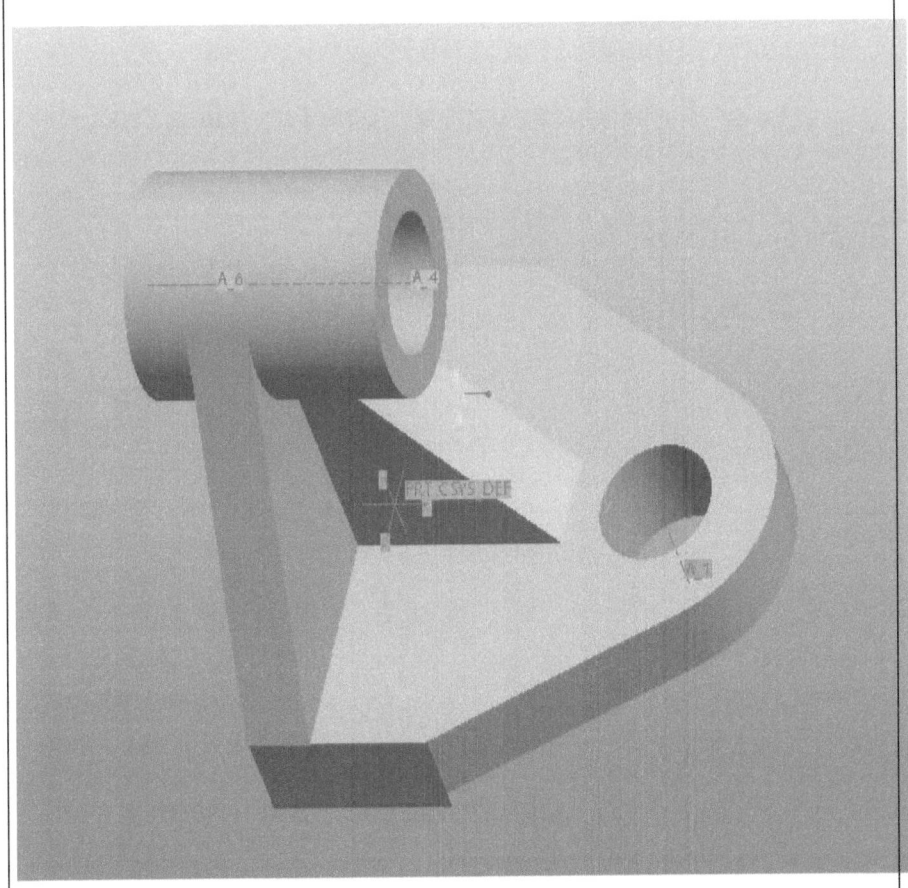

# SOLID MODELING OF SUPPORT BRACKET

**Aim:**

To draw the given support bracket by using Pro/E software.

**Software used:**

- Pro/E Wildfire version 4.0

**Commands used:**

- Line
- Extrude
- Rib

**Procedure:**

**Step 1:**

- Open Pro/E wildfire version 4.0 software
- Set working directory
- File-new-part
- Change the template into **mmns part solid**

**Step2:**

- Insert-extrude-placement-define-top plane
- Sketch the rectangle of 46x116 and click ok.
- It is extruded up to a distance of 20 mm below top plane & click ok.

- Part 1 is created.

**Step3:**

- Insert-extrude-placement-define-top plane
- Draw the sketch by using suitable reference object to be extruded should be closed sketch.
- Now, the extrusion of 16 mm from top plane is given & click ok.

# SUPPORT BRACKET

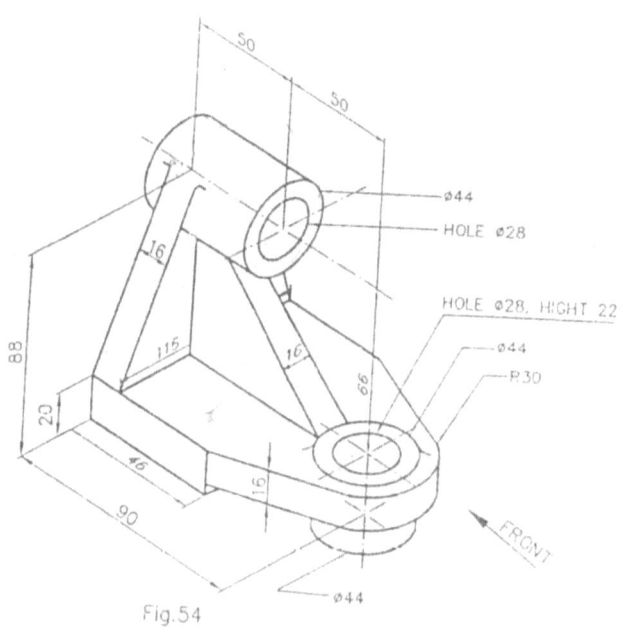

Fig.54

**Step4:**

- Insert-extrude-placement-define-use previous plane
- By sketching tool draw two circle of diameter 44&28 mm respectively.
- Extrude it below top plane to a distance of 22mm & click ok.

**Step5:**

- Insert-extrude-placement-define-left side surface
- Sketch two circle of diameter 44 & 28 mm at a distance of 68 mm from top plane.
- Extrude it up to a distance 40 mm on edge side of 40 mm 0n back side. It is done by using option in near to placement at extrude command us to blind to both extrude side & click ok.

**Step6:**

- A connection between cylinder & rectangle block is drawn by insert-extrude-placement
- Define the previous plane & connect the part by line tool.
- Now extrude it by giving 16 mm of value.

**Step7:**

- Insert-rib-profile trajectory
- Select any reference a line connections two reference. It should be closed. Flip is required sided & give a thickness of 16 mm.

**Result:**

Thus, the given solid modeling of support bracket is drawn with the given dimensions by using Pro/E software.

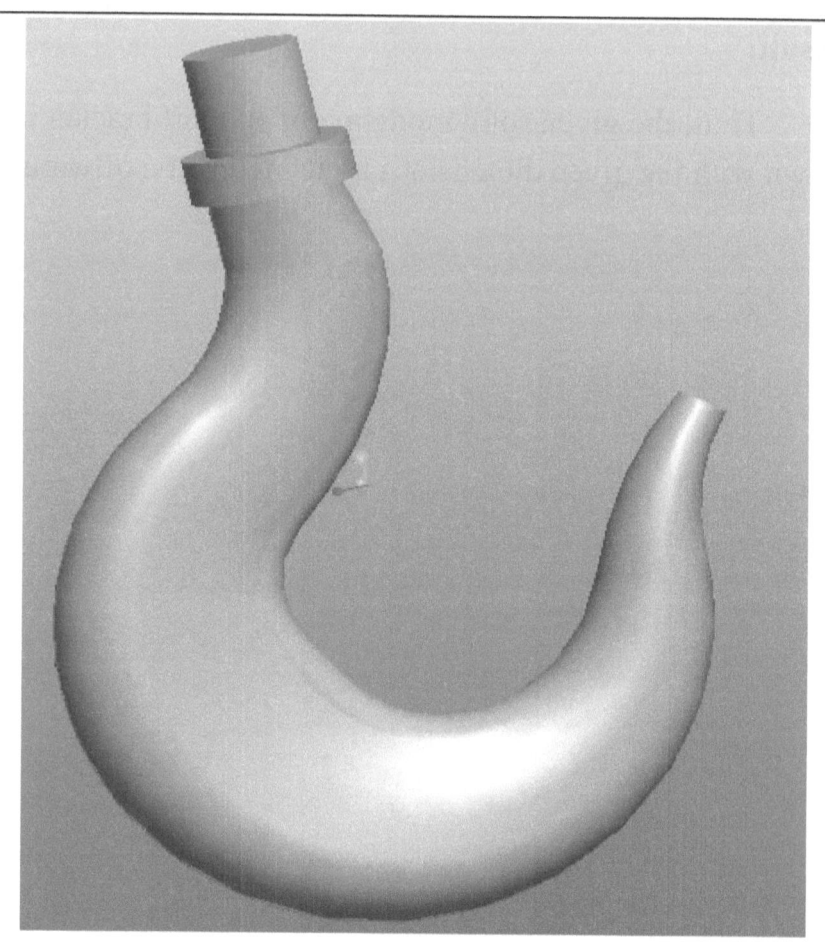

# CRANE HOOK

# CRANE HOOK

**Aim:**

To draw the given Crane hook diagram by using the Pro-E software.

**Software used:**

- Pro-E wildfire 4.0

**Commands used:**

- Sketch tools→ circle, rectangle, line, trim
- Extrude
- Swept blend

**Procedure:**

- Open the Pro-E wildfire 4.0
- Set working directory.
- select a file→ new→ part
- Select part and unmark the default template for using S.I. units in **mmns part solid**
- A window to draw the object will appear.

**Step 1:**

- Select the command sketch→ placement→ define→ front plane.
- Select right orientation.
- Sketch a circle of radius 150 mm.
- Trim top left side (II quadrant) of circle.
- Draw an arc of radius of 75mm which connects a point(30×188) and top edge of circle
- Draw another arc of 100mm at bottom edges of the circle to the height of 65mm and click ok.

**Step 2:**

- Select the command insert→ swept blend.

- Select the trajectory.
- Create a two datum points as per the given drawing.
- Choose the section option and select the start point and draw a circle of radius 30mm and divide it into 4 using divide tool and Click ok.

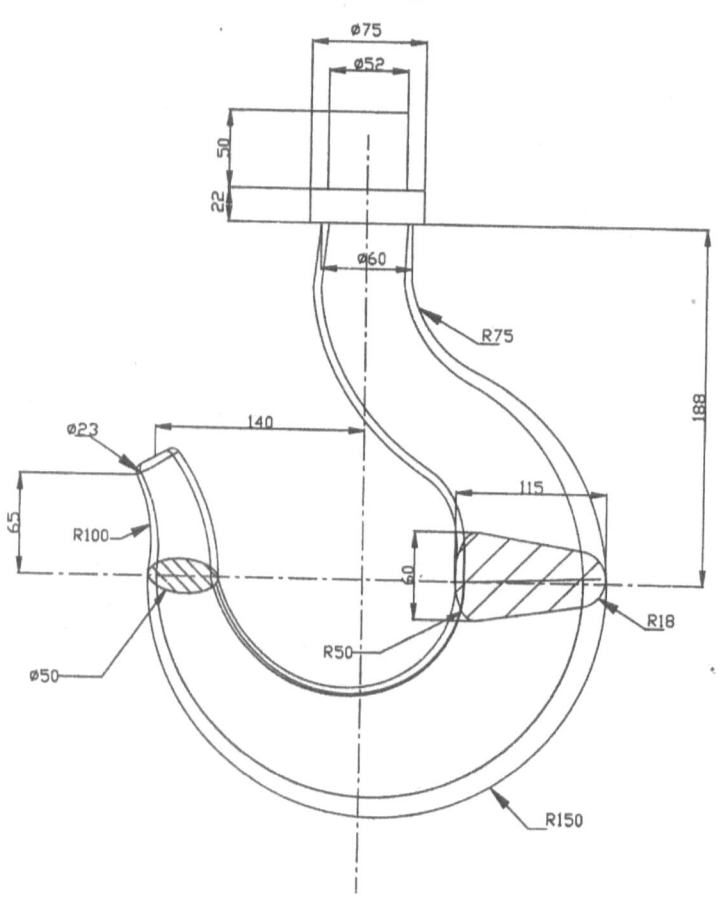

**ALL DIMESIONS ARE IN MM**

- Click insert.
- Now, choose the second point and click sketch.
- Draw a circle of radius of 25 mm and divide it into 4 using divide tool and click ok.
- Click insert.
- Now, choose the third point and click sketch.
- Draw the given element as per the section in the drawing and divide it into 4 using divide tool and click ok.
- Click insert.
- Now, choose the end point and click sketch.
- Draw a circle of radius of 15 mm and divide it into 4 using divide tool and click ok.

**Extrude:**

- Select the command insert→ extrude→ placement→ define→ top plane with right orientation.
- Draw two circle of radius of 26mm, 37.5mm and click ok.
- Extrude to a distance of 22 mm and click ok.

**Result:**

Thus the given crane hook is drawn with the dimensions by using PRO E software.

# ASSEMBLY OF KNUCKLE JOINT

**Aim:**

To assemble the parts of a knuckle joint using Pro/E software.

**Software used:**

- Pro/E wildfire version 4.0

**Commands used:**

- Extrude
- Revolve
- Revolve cut
- Mirror

**Procedure:**

- Open Pro/E software
- Set the working directory
- File→ New → Part
- Remove the tick mark to change default template into **mmns part solid.**

**Part 1:**

**Step 1:**

- Select the extrude command
- Extrude→ Placement→ Define→ Top plane
- Sketch the rectangle as per the given diagram and sketch two circle at left of the rectangle.

- Join the rectangle and two circles with tangent curve
- Now the section will be closed and click ok
- Sketch is extruded up to 30 mm.

## KNUCKLE JOINT

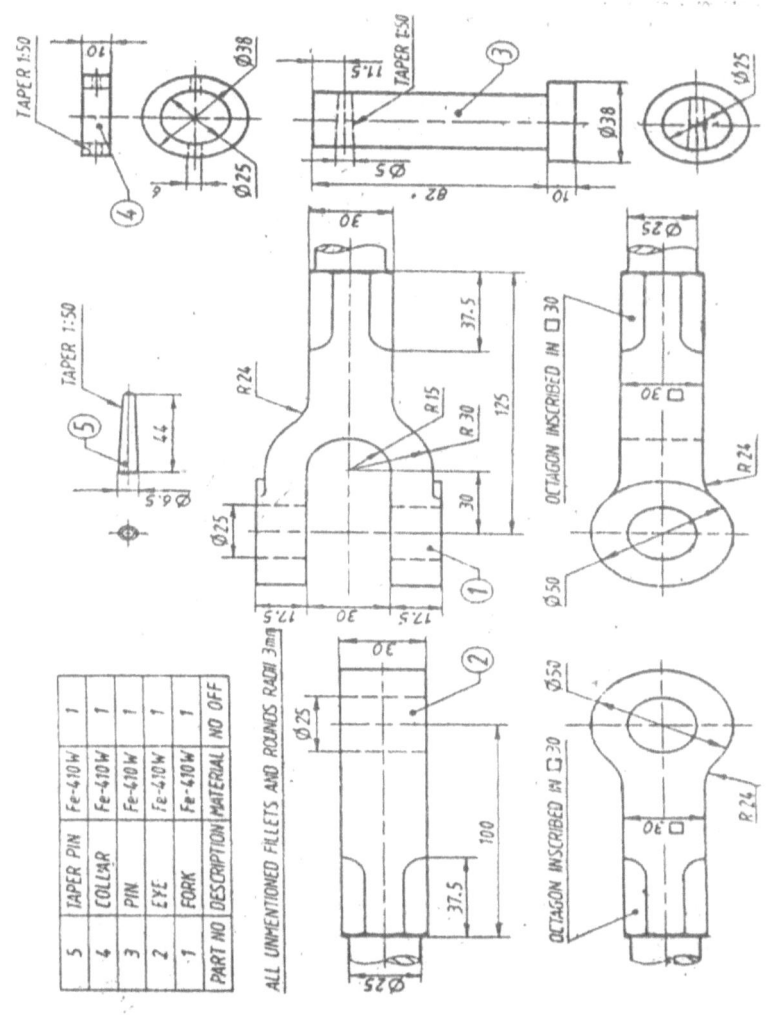

# ALL DIMESIONS ARE IN MM

# KNUCKLE JOINT

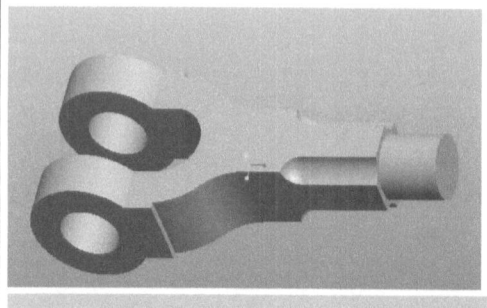

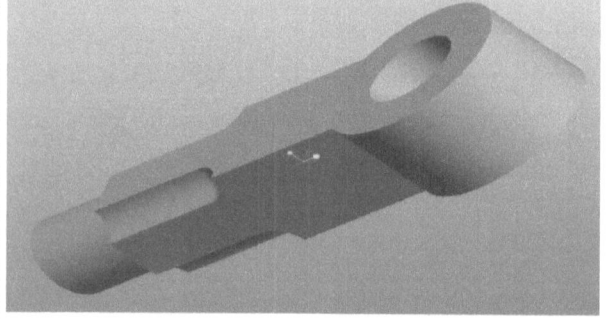

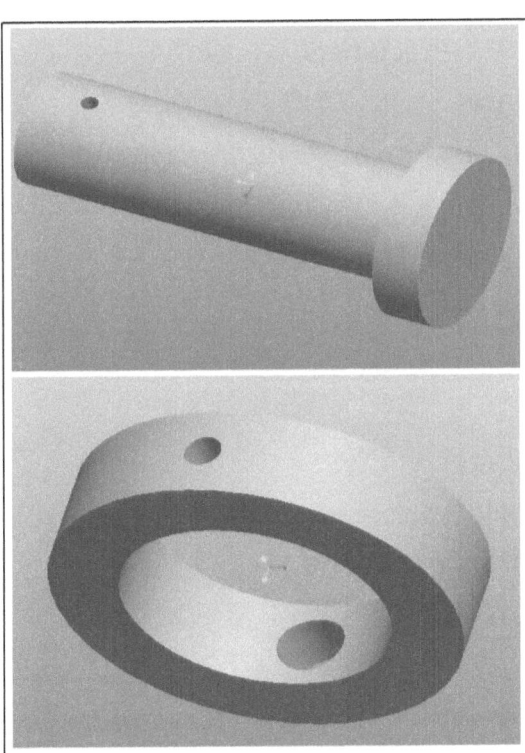

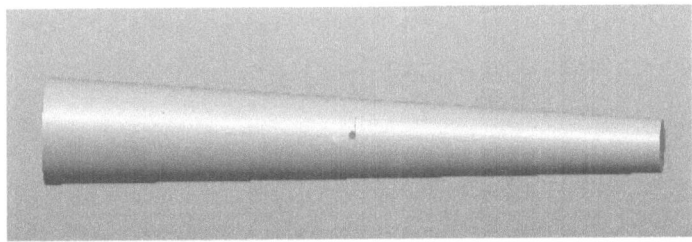

## Step 2:

- Select Extrude→ Placement→ Define→ Front surface of the object
- Sketch a circle and extrude up to a small length which is for the shaft extension.

## Step 3:

- Select Revolve→ Placement→ Define→ Top surface of the object
- Sketch the section shown in figure and revolve around 360°
- Select remove material and click ok.
- Save the part.

## Part 2:

- File→ New→ Part
- Remove the tick mark to change in default template into **mmns part solid.**

## Step 1:

- Extrude→ Placement→ Define→ Front plane
- Sketch the rectangle and also sketch two circles as per the given diagram
- Join the rectangle and two circles as shown in figure.
- Sketch is extruded up to 30 mm.

## Step 2:

- Extrude→ Placement→ Define→ Top surface of the object
- Sketch the two circles and join with the above object.
- Sketch is extruded up to 17.5 mm

## Step 3:

Select the revolve command

- Revolve→ Placement → Define→ Second top surface of the object
- Sketch the section as per the given diagram
- Sketch is revolved for 360° and select move material

**Step 4:**

- Select the second extruded object
- Select the mirror command
- Select object middle plane between first object and then click ok

**Step 5:**

- Extrude→ Placement→ Define→ Front surface of the object
- Sketch the circle and is extruded
- Save the part.

**Part 3:**

- Click File→ New→ Part
- Remove the tick mark to change in default template into **mmns part solid.**

**Step 1:**

- Extrude→ Placement→ Define→ Top plane
- Sketch the circle of diameter 25 mm and extruded up to 82 mm.

**Step 2:**

- Extrude→ Placement→ Define→ Top surface of the object
- Sketch the circle of diameter 38 mm and is extruded up to 10 mm

**Step 3:**

- Revolve→ Placement→ Define→ Front plane
- Sketch the section as per the given diagram and revolve around 360°
- Select remove material

**Part 4:**

- Click File→ New→ Part
- Remove the tick mark to change in default template into **mmns part solid.**

**Step 1:**

- Insert → Extrude → Placement → Define → Select the top plane.
- Sketch the two circles and extrude up to 10mm.

### KNUCKLE JOINT

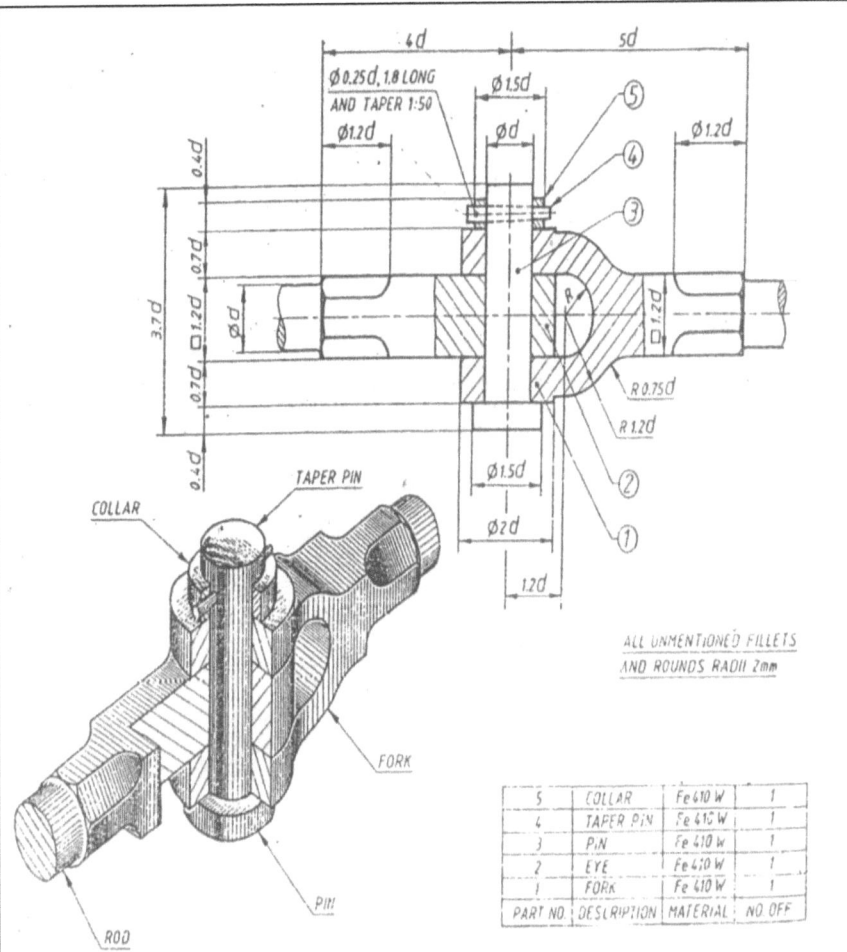

ALL UNMENTIONED FILLETS
AND ROUNDS RADII 2mm

| 5 | COLLAR | Fe 410 W | 1 |
| 4 | TAPER PIN | Fe 410 W | 1 |
| 3 | PIN | Fe 410 W | 1 |
| 2 | EYE | Fe 410 W | 1 |
| 1 | FORK | Fe 410 W | 1 |
| PART NO. | DESCRIPTION | MATERIAL | NO. OFF |

TAPER PIN

COLLAR

FORK

PIN

ROD

**ALL DIMENSIONS ARE IN MM**

**KNUCKLE JOINT**

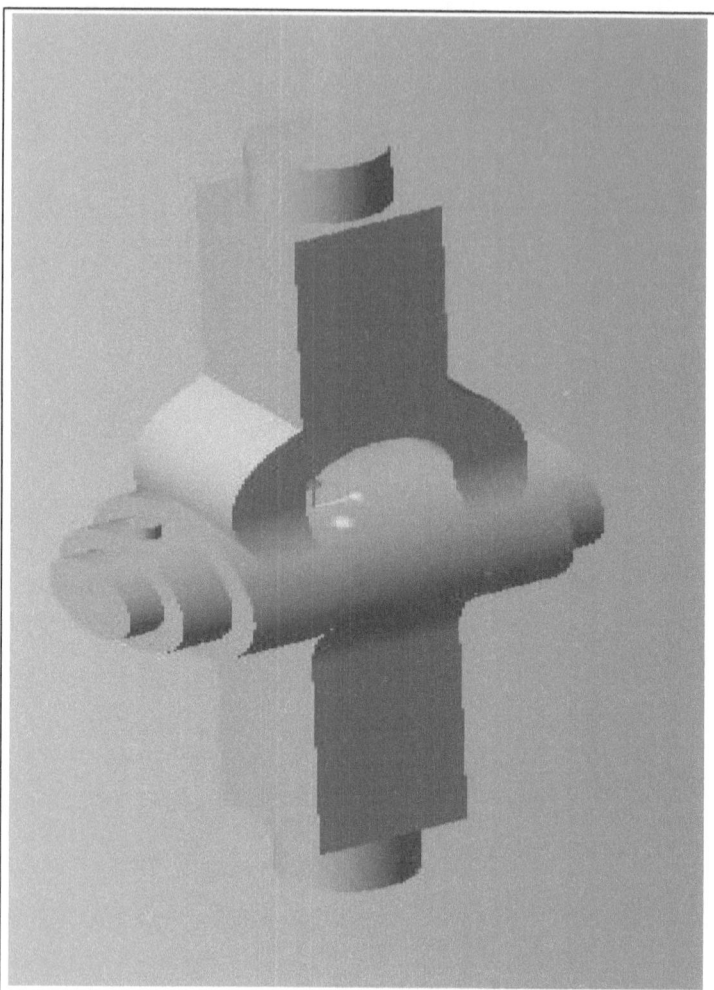

**Step2:**

- Insert → Extrude → Placement → Define → Select the front plane.
- Sketch the section and revolve for 360°.
- Select remove material.
- Save the part and close the window.

**Part5:**

- Click File→ New→ Part

- Remove the tick mark to change in default template into **mmns part solid.**

## Step1:

- Click Insert → Extrude → Placement → Define → Select the front plane.
- Sketch the section and revolve it to 360°
- Save the part.

## Assembly:

## Constraints used:

- Automatic
- Align
- Mate
- Point on surface
- Insert
- Fix

## Assembly of fork:

- Select assemble → part → fork part
- Select the constraint as default to create it as base object. Click ok.

## Assembly of eye:

- Select assemble → part → eye part
- Select the constraint as mate and join the top surface of eye to inner top surface of the fork.

- Select the new constraint as mate and select the two side surfaces of object and give the angle 180°

## Assembly of pin:

- Select assemble → part → pin part
- Select the constraint as align and join the axis of pin and axis of fork.
- Select the new constraint as mate and join the bottom of fork and bottom of pin.
- Now, the pin will be fully constrained.

## Assembly of collar:

- Select assemble → part → collar part
- Select the constraint as align and join the axis of pin and axis of collar.
- Select the new constraint as mate and join bottom surface of collar and top surface of fork.

## Assembly of taper pin:

- Select assemble → part → taper pin part
- Select the constraint as align and join the axis of taper pin and axis of pin.
- Now, the assembly of knuckle joint is done.
- Save the assembly.

## Result:

Thus, the assembly of knuckle joint is done with given dimensions using by Pro/E software.

# ASSEMBLY OF FLANGED COUPLING

**Aim:**

To assemble the parts of a flanged coupling using PRO-E software

**Software used:**

- Pro/E wildfire version 4.0

**Commands used:**

- Extrude cut
- Extrude
- Pattern
- Helical sweep

**Procedure:**

- Open PRO-E software
- Set the working directory

**Part1:**

**Step1:**

- File→ new → part
- Remove the tick mark and change default template to mmns.
- Extrude → placement → define → front plane
- Sketch the circle of diameter 190 mm .

- Sketch 4 circle of diameter 12mm as per dimensions.
- Sketch is extruded up to 20mm and click ok.

**Step2:**

- Click insert→ extrude→ placement→ front plane.
- Sketch the circle of diameter 90 mm.
- Sketch is extruded up to 75 mm and click ok.

FLANGED COUPLING

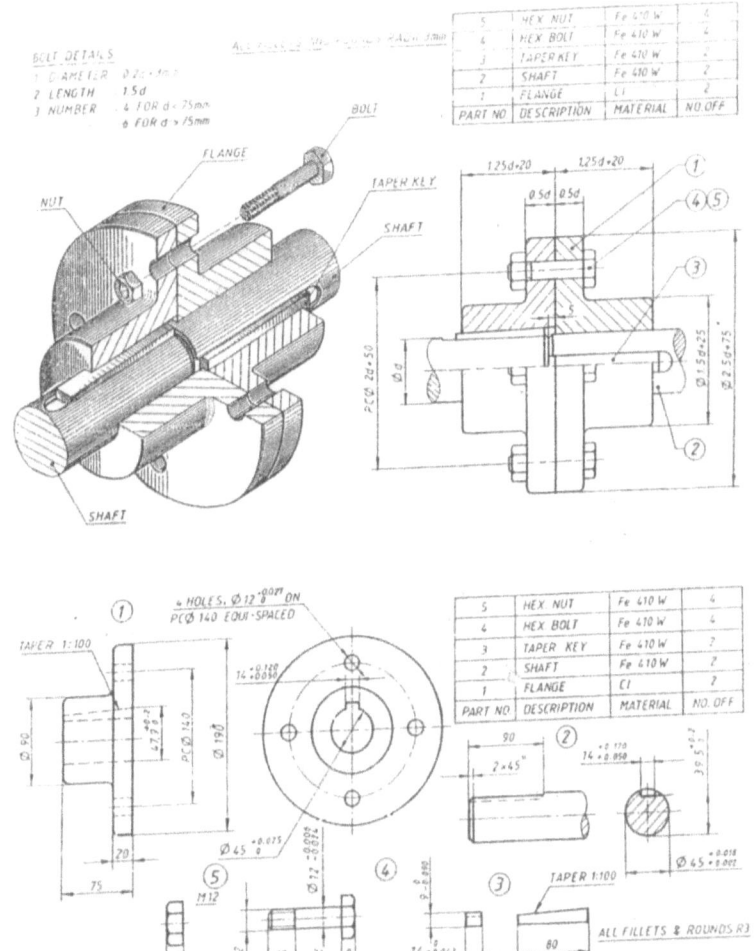

**ALL DIMENSIONS ARE IN MM**

**FLANGED COUPLING**

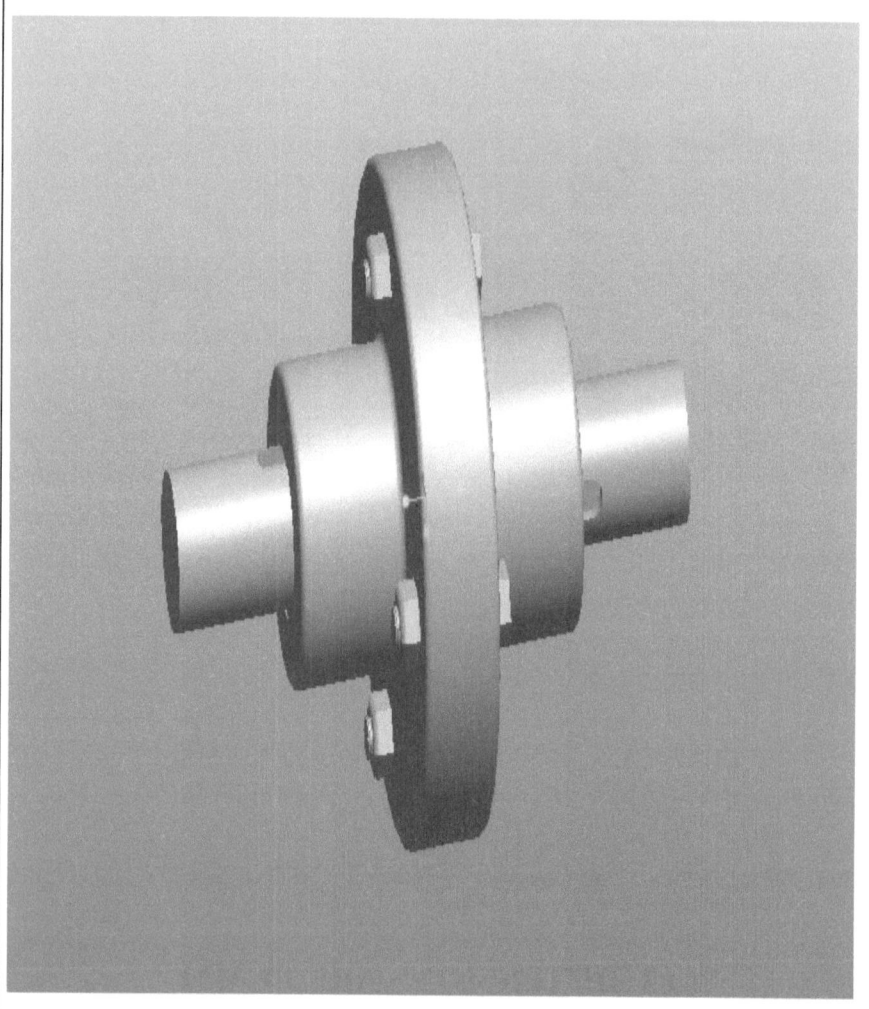

## Step3:

- Select insert→ extrude→ placement→ define→ front surface.
- Sketch a circle of diameter 45mm.

- Select "remove material' and extrude cut up to 75mm and click ok.

**Step4:**

- Click insert→ extrude→ placement→ define→ right plane.
- Sketch the section as per the dimensions.
- Select the remove material and extrude the cut up to 12 mm and click ok.

**Part 2:**

- File→ new → part
- Remove the tick mark and change default template to mmns

**Step1:**

- Select extrude command.
- Extrude→ placement→ define→ front plane.
- Sketch a circle of 45 mm.
- Sketch is extruded up to 135mm and click ok.

**Step2:**

- First datum plane is created parallel to top plane up to the distance of 22.5mm.
- Select extrude command.
- Extrude→ placement→ define→ define datum plane.
- Sketch rectangle 20mm height and 90mm length.
- Select remove material and extrude cut 7mm and click ok.

# Part3:

- File→ new → part
- Remove the tick mark and change default template to mmns
- Select extrude command.

Select extrude→ placement → define→ front plane

### FLANGED COUPLING

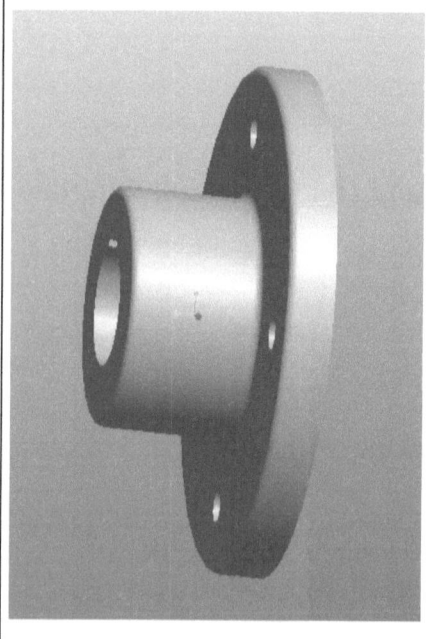
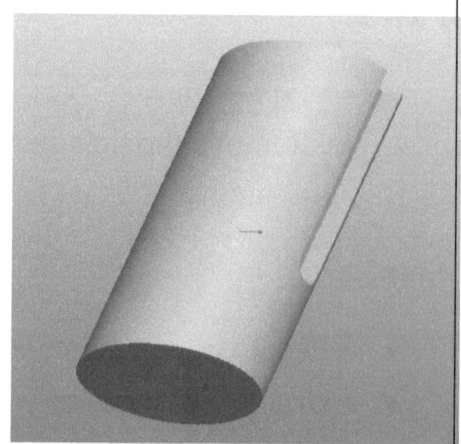

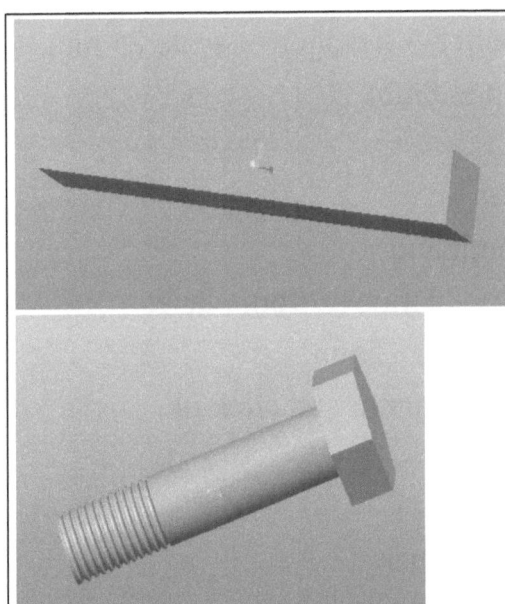

- Sketch a taper key as per dimensions.
- Sketch is extruded up to 12mm and click ok.
- Save and close window.

**Part 4:**

- File→ new → part
- Remove the tick mark and change default template to mmns

**Step1:**

- Sketch the model using extrude command.
- Extrude → placement→ define→ front plane

- Select the sketcher pallet→ hexagon→ scale 25 mm.
- Sketch is extruded up to 8mm.

**Step2:**

- Select the extrude command.
- Extrude→ placement→ define→ front plane.
- Sketch a circle of diameter 12mm.
- Sketch is extruded up to 60mm and click ok.

**Step3:**

- Select helical sweep command.
- Helical sweep→ thin cut→ right plane.
- Sweep profile, center axis is created.
- Draw a line of 18mm and click ok.
- Enter a pitch value is 15mm.
- Next draw a circle of diameter 1 mm and click ok.
- Helical sweep is created.

**Part5:**

**Step1:**

- Select the extrude command.
- Extrude→ placement → define → front plane.
- Select sketcher pallet→ hexagon → 25mm.
- Sketch is extruded up to 10mm and ok.

**Step2:**

- Select extrude command.
- Extrude→ placement→ define→ front plane.

- Sketch a circle diameter of 12mm,
- Sketch is extruded up to 10mm with remove material and click ok.

## Step3:

- Select a helical sweep command.
- Helical sweep→ thin cut → select the right plane.
- Sweep profile→ centre axis is created, draw a line 10mm and click ok.
- Next draw a circle of diameter of 1mm and helical sweep is created.

## Assembly:

## Constraints used:

- Automatic
- Align
- Mate
- Insert
- Fix

## Assembly of flange:

- Select the assemble → part→ flange part
- Select the constraint as default to create it as base object.
- Now the flange will be fully constrained.

## Assembly of shaft:

- Select the assemble → part→ shaft part

- Select the new constraint as align and join the axis of shaft and axis of flange.
- Shaft will be fully constrained.

## Assembly of taper key:

- Select the assemble → part→ taper key part
- Select the new constraint as mate and join the top surface of the taper key and top surface of the shaft.

## Assembly of hexagonal bolt:

- Select the assemble → part→ hexagonal bolt part
- Select the new constraint as align and join the axis of bolt and axis of flange in small circle
- Select the new constraint as mate and join the bottom of front surface in flange.

## Assembly of hexagonal nut:

- Select the assemble → part→ hexagonal nut part
- Select the new constraint as align and join the bolt axis and nut axis.
- Select the new constraint as mate and join the bottom of front surface in nut and bottom of front surface in flange.
- Now the hexagonal nut will be fully constrained.
- Now the assembly of flanged coupling is done
- Save the assembly.

## Result:

Thus, the assembly of flanged coupling is done with given dimensions using by Pro/E software.

# ASSEMBLY OF SCREW JACK

**Aim:**

      To assemble the parts of a screw jack by using Pro-E software.

**Software used:**

- Pro-E Wildfire V4.0

**Commands used:**

- Extrude
- Revolve
- Helical sweep

**Procedure:**

- Open the Pro-E software.
- Set the working directory.
- File → New→ Part
- Remove the tick mark and set the default template as mmns.

**Part1:**

- Click insert→ Revolve→ Placement→ Define
- Front plane is selected.
- Sketch the cutter shape of the body as per the given dimension.

- Sketch is revolved at 360°.
- Click OK and save the part.

**Part 2:**

- File → New→ Part
- Remove the tick mark and the change the default template to mmns.
- Click→ Revolve→ Placement→ Define
- Front plane is selected.

## SCREW JACK

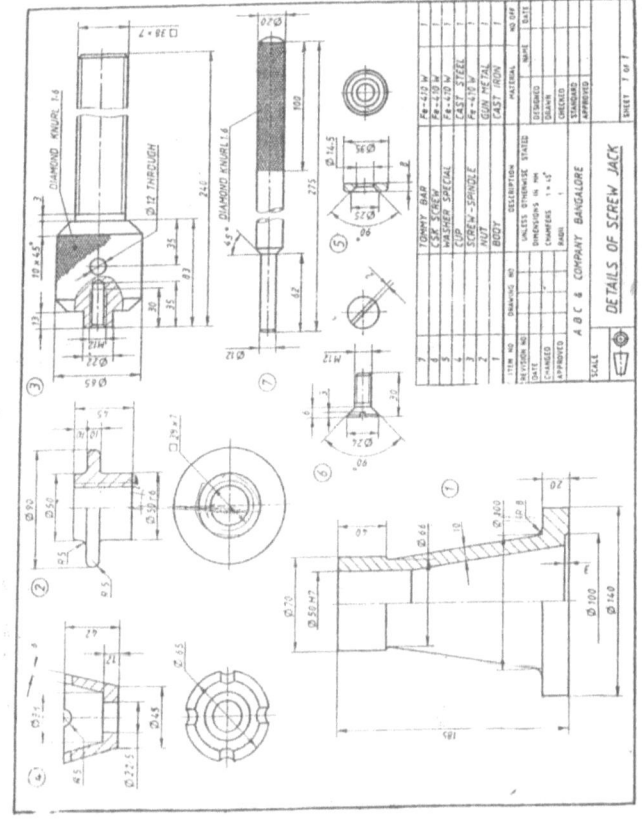

# ALL DIMENSIONS ARE IN MM

- Sketch a rectangle of dimension 25mm×45mm.
- Sketch a diagram as per the given dimension.
- Sketch is revolved at 360º.
- Click OK and save the part.

## Part 3:

## Step1:

- File → New→ Part
- Remove the tick mark and change default template to mmns.
- Click Insert→ Revolve→ Placement→ Define.
- Front plane is selected.
- Sketch the section as per the given dimension.
- Sketch is revolved at 360º.
- Click OK and save the part.

## Step2:

- Select the extrude command.
- Extrude → Placement→ Define.
- Front plane is selected.
- Sketch a circle of diameter 38mm.
- Sketch is extruded up to 157mm.
- Click OK and save the part.

## Part 3:

- Select helical sweep command.

- Helical sweep → Thin cut→ Select a plane.
- Sweep profile → Centre axis is created, draw a line of length 157mm and then click OK.
- Enter a pitch value of 1.5mm.
- Next draw a circle of diameter 15mm and then click OK.
- Helical sweep is created.
- Save the part.

## SCREW JACK

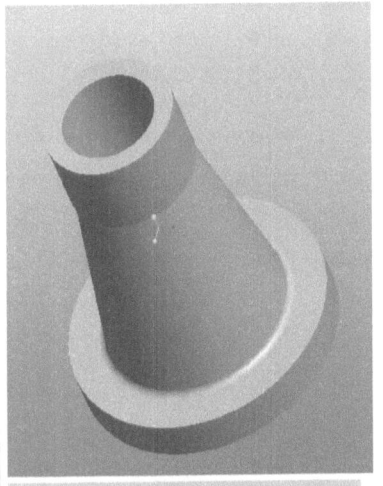

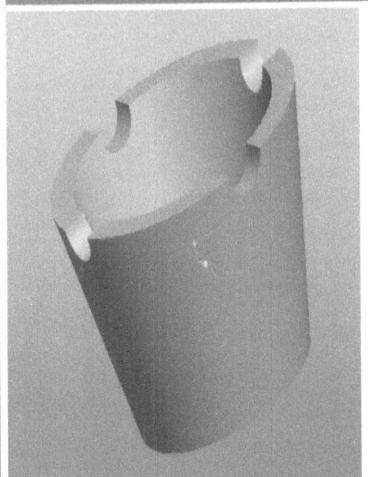

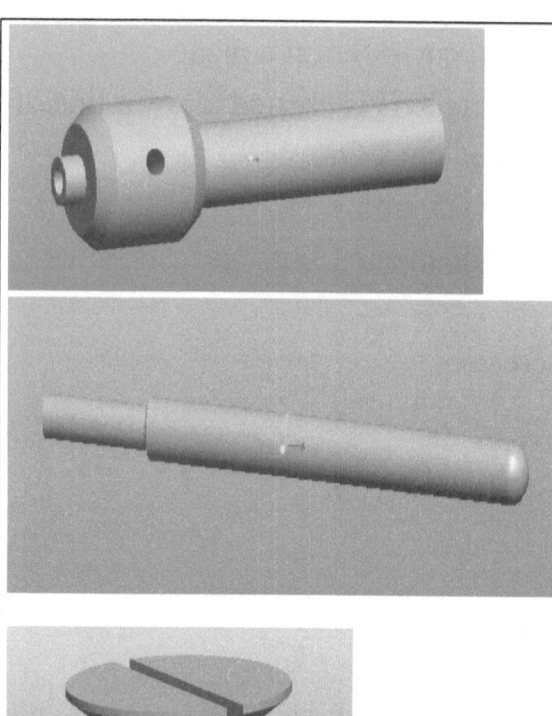

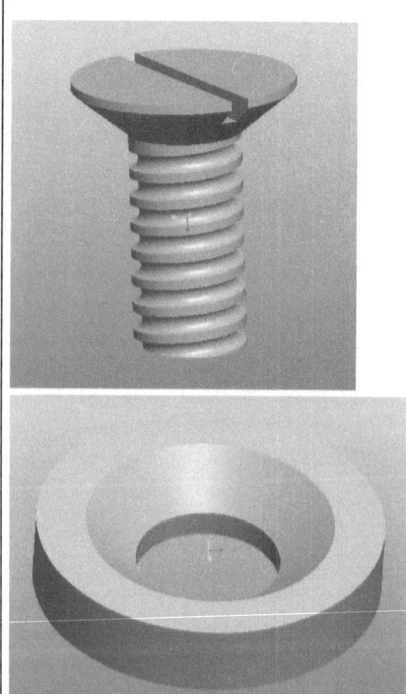

**Part 4:**

- File → New→ Part
- Remove the tick mark to change the default template into mmns.
- Revolve→ Placement→ Define.
- Front plane is selected.
- Sketch the section as per the given dimension.
- Sketch is revolved at 360°.
- Click OK and save the part.

## Part 5:

- File → New→ Part
- Remove the tick mark to change the default template into mmns.
- Select the remove command.
- Extrude → Placement→ Define.
- Front plane is selected.
- Sketch the circles of diameter 25mm and 35mm.
- Sketch is extruded up to 8mm.
- Click OK and save the part.

## Part 6:

- File → New→ Part
- Remove the tick mark to change the default template into mmns.
- Select the remove command.
- Revolve → Placement→ Define.
- Front plane is selected.
- Sketch the given section as per the given dimension.

- Sketch is revolved at 360º.
- Click OK and save the part.

**Step 2:**

- Select the extrude command.

## SCREW JACK

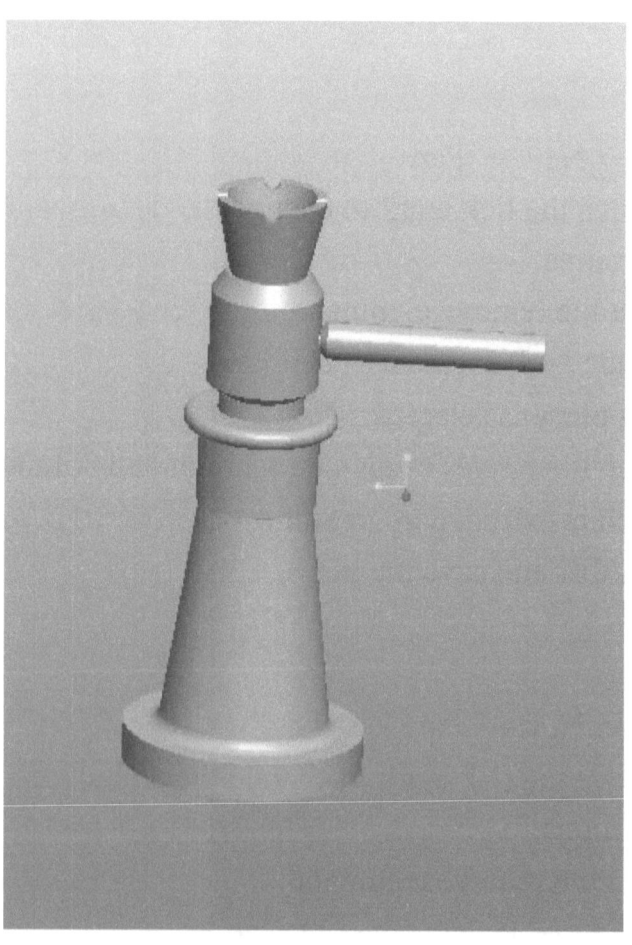

- Extrude → Placement→ Define
- Front plane is selected.
- Sketch a circle of diameter 12mm.
- Sketch is extruded up to 24mm.
- Click OK and save the part.

**Step 3:**

- Select a helical sweep command.
- Helical sweep→ thin cut→ Select a plane.
- Sweep profile→ centre axis is created, draw a line of length 24mm and click OK.
- Enter a pitch value of 1.5mm.
- Next draw a circle of diameter 1mm and then click OK.
- Helical sweep is created.
- Save the part.

**Part 7:**

**Step1:**

- File → New→ Part
- Remove the tick mark to change the default template into mmns.
- Select the remove command.
- Extrude → Placement→ Define→ Front plane.
- Sketch a circle of diameter 12mm and click OK.
- Sketch is extruded up to 62 mm .
- Save the part.

**Step2:**

- Select extrude command.
- Extrude → Placement→ Define→ Front plane.
- Sketch a circle of diameter 20mm.
- Sketch is extruded up to 213mm and click OK.
- Next diamond knurl is created up to 100 mm.

## ASSEMBLY OF SCREW JACK

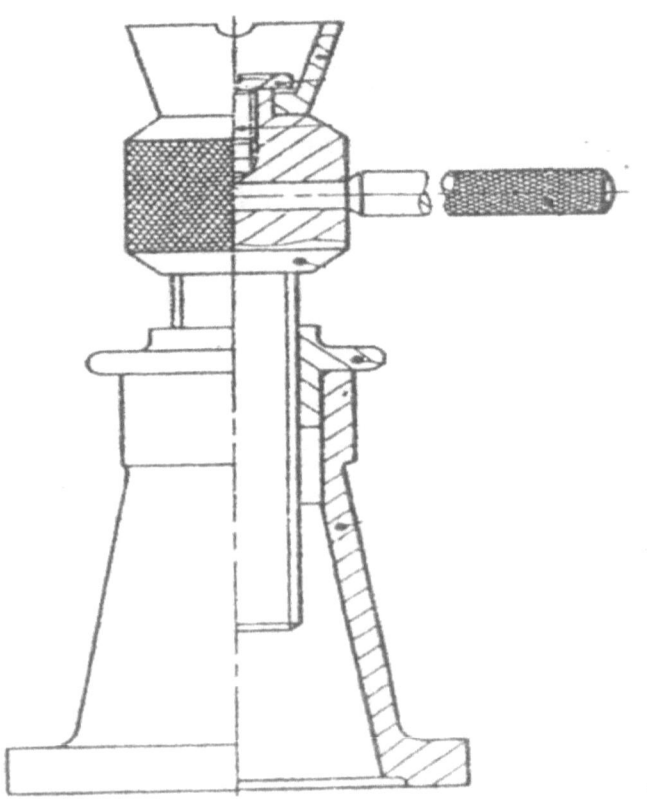

**ALL DIMENSIONS ARE IN MM**

**Assembly**

**Constraints used:**

- Automatic
- Align
- Mate
- Insert
- Fix

**Assembly of body:**

- Select the assemble → part → body part
- Select the constraint as default to create it as base point
- Now the body will be fully constrained.

**Assembly of nut:**

- Select the assemble → part → nut part
- Select a new constraint as align and join the axis of the body and axis of the nut.
- Now the nut will be fully constrained.

**Assembly of screw spindle:**

- Select the assemble → part → screw spindle part
- Select new constraint as align and join the axis of nut and axis of body.
- Now the screw spindle will be fully constrained.

## Assemble of cup:

- Select the assemble → part → cup part
- Select the new constraint as align and join the axis of cup and axis of the body.
- Select a new constraint as mate and join the front surface of screw spindle and front surface of cup.

## Assembly of washer special:

- Select assemble → part → washer special part
- Select new constraint as align & join the axis of washer special & axis of cup.
- Select the new constraint as mate & join the front surface of washer special and front surface of cup.
- Now, the washer special will be fully constrained.

## Assembly of CSK Screw:

- Select assemble → part→ csk screw
- Select the new constraint as align and join the axis of csk screw and axis of washer.
- Select the new constraint as mate & join the bottom of front surface in csk screw and front surface of washer.
- Now, the csk screw will be fully constrained.

## Assembly of tommy bar:

- Select the assemble → part → tommy bar part
- Select the new constraint as align and join the axis of the screw spindle and axis of the tommy bar.
- Now the tommy bar will be fully constrained.

- Now the assembly of screw jack is done
- Save the assembly.

## Result:

Thus, the assembly of screw jack is done with given dimensions by using Pro/E software.